BREAKFAST BY CANDLELIGHT
DEDICATION

I wrote this book in honor of my two children, Steve and Kelli, who are now grown adults! When Steve and Kelli were growing up, I served them breakfast by candlelight most every morning! It did not matter that they had to get ready for school early. I always made sure I had breakfast ready for them and that the candles were glowing. I hope this book brings back special memories for my two very special children.

ALL MY LOVE,

Mom

Breakfast by Candlelight

WRITTEN BY
LORI MATTICE

ILLUSTRATED BY JAN SHANNON

It's Monday morning. Steve and Kelli are fast asleep.
Meanwhile, in the kitchen downstairs,
their mother is preparing a special treat.
What special breakfast will they awaken to today?
It's sure to be wonderful in every way.

BLUEBERRY SMILEY FACE PANCAKES

1 cup whole wheat pancake mix
1 cup milk
1 tablespoon vegetable oil
1 egg
Fresh blueberries

- Heat skillet over medium-low heat or electric griddle to 375 degrees
- Combine all ingredients (except blueberries) and stir until large lumps disappear (do not overmix). Let stand for 1-2 minutes to thicken
- Pour 1/4 cup of batter for each pancake onto lightly greased skillet
- Arrange blueberries on top of the pancake into a smiley face
- Turn when pancakes bubble and bottoms are golden brown

Serve with warm blueberry syrup and butter!

Steve and Kelli creep down the stairs
and before they can count to three,
the candlelight glow is the first thing they see.
Today a pancake with a blueberry smiley face fills their plate.
As warm syrup is poured, they agree it is the best they ever ate.

Breakfast by candlelight starts the morning just right!

Tuesday morning comes all too fast.
Steve and Kelli will discover
their breakfast
surprise at
last.

The table is set with colorful napkins;
the candles glowing ever so bright.
They enjoy the "heart-tee" egg sandwich
to the very last bite.

HEART-TEE EGG SANDWICH

2 slices wheat or white sandwich bread
(buttered on both sides)
2 eggs
Heart shaped cookie cutter
Salt and pepper to taste
Pam spray

- Use cookie cutter to cut heart shape in the middle of the bread
- Butter both sides of the bread
- Spray Pam on skillet
- Place 2 pieces of bread in skillet over medium heat
- Crack egg into the heart shape in bread - cook to desired doneness
- Flip the bread over and cook on the other side until golden brown
- Salt and pepper to taste
- Sides: Crispy bacon and orange juice

Now off to school they go, ready, eager faces aglow.

Breakfast by candlelight starts the morning just right!

Wednesday, a fruit and yogurt parfait greets the kids as they make their way to the kitchen. The glow of the candlelight catches their eyes, to remind them that breakfast time can be a surprise.

FRUIT AND YOGURT PARFAIT
(4 servings)

4 tall glasses
3 cups vanilla yogurt
1 cup fresh strawberries
1/2 cup fresh blueberries
1/2 cup raspberries
1/2 cup blackberries
1/2 cup sliced bananas
1/2 cup cantaloupe cubed
1 cup good quality granola

- Layer 1/3 cup vanilla yogurt in the bottom of each of the 4 tall glasses
- Combine all fresh fruit (make sure all fruit is washed and sliced if necessary)
- Alternate layers of the fruit and granola with the yogurt until glasses are filled to the top (sprinkle additional granola on top)
- Serve immediately so the granola stays crunchy

Bananas, strawberries, cantaloupe and more, eating fruit this way is never a bore!

Breakfast by candlelight starts the morning just right!

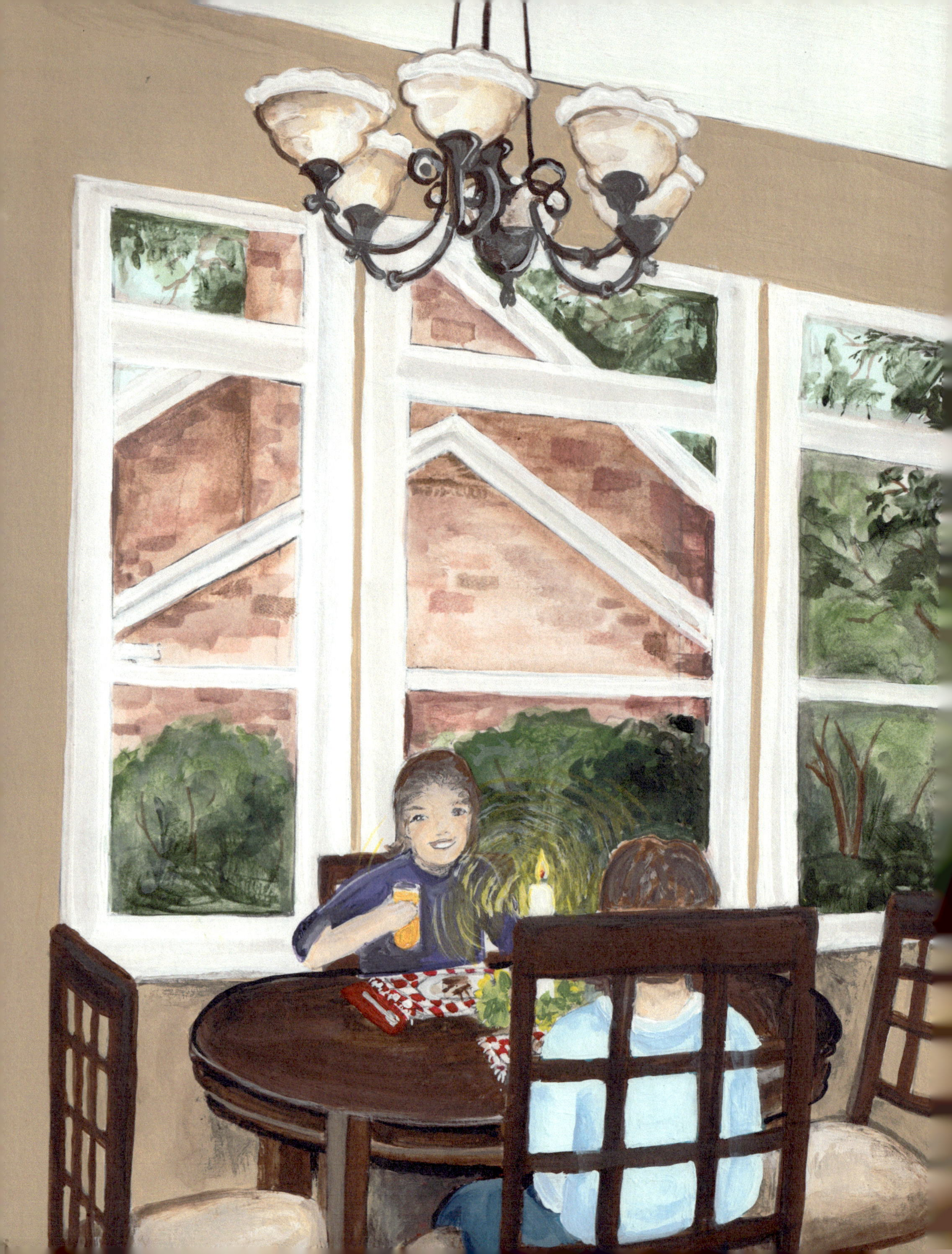

Thursday morning has arrived
with the candles in place,
Steve and Kelli see their breakfast
with a smile on their face.

French toast sticks
with lots of powdered sugar
will make them flip,
As into the warm syrup
each piece they dip.

Breakfast by candlelight starts the morning just right!

FRENCH TOAST STICKS

4 slices wheat or white bread
3 eggs
1 teaspoon butter
1 tablespoon milk
Powdered sugar
Maple syrup heated

- Crack 3 eggs into a mixing bowl
- Add milk
- Whisk eggs and milk together
- Heat butter in skillet
- Dip bread into egg mixture soaking egg mixture on both sides of bread
- Place bread into skillet and cook French toast until golden brown on both sides
- Remove from heat, cut bread into 4 sticks (slices)
- Place on plate, sprinkle powdered sugar over French toast sticks and dip the sticks into the warm maple syrup

It's Friday morning at last. Steve and Kelli wonder what surprise awaits them today.
Please tell them fast!
It's chocolate chip waffles on their plates,
One of their favorites, oh they can't wait!

(Steve and Kelli's "Gran", who loves to cook, would often participate in helping to prepare the candlelight breakfast.)

CHOCOLATE CHIP WAFFLES
(Makes six 4" waffles)

Waffle maker
Pam spray
Pancake Mix (wheat or white)
Ghirardelli Premium Baking Grand Sweet Chocolate Chips
Whipped cream in spray bottle
1 1/4 cups milk
1 egg
3 tablespoons vegetable oil

- Heat waffle iron
- Combine 1 1/4 cup pancake mix with 1 1/4 cups milk, 1 egg and 3 tablespoons vegetable oil
- Stir until large clumps disappear
- Allow batter to rest 4-5 minutes before baking
- Pour 1/4 cup of batter into lightly greased waffle iron
- Bake until steaming stops
- Take waffles out of waffle iron and transfer to plate
- Sprinkle chocolate chips on top of waffle followed by a few squirts of whipped cream
- Serve with syrup and butter if desired

Breakfast by candlelight starts the morning just right!

Ah, the weekend is here,
It seemed so fast,
they wanted to cheer.
This Saturday morning,
what will be in store?
But wait, Steve and Kelli
want to sleep a little more.

And as they awake,
they know that their breakfast
will be ready soon.

The smell of sausage floats up to their rooms.

SAUSAGE, PEANUT BUTTER AND JELLY BISCUITS

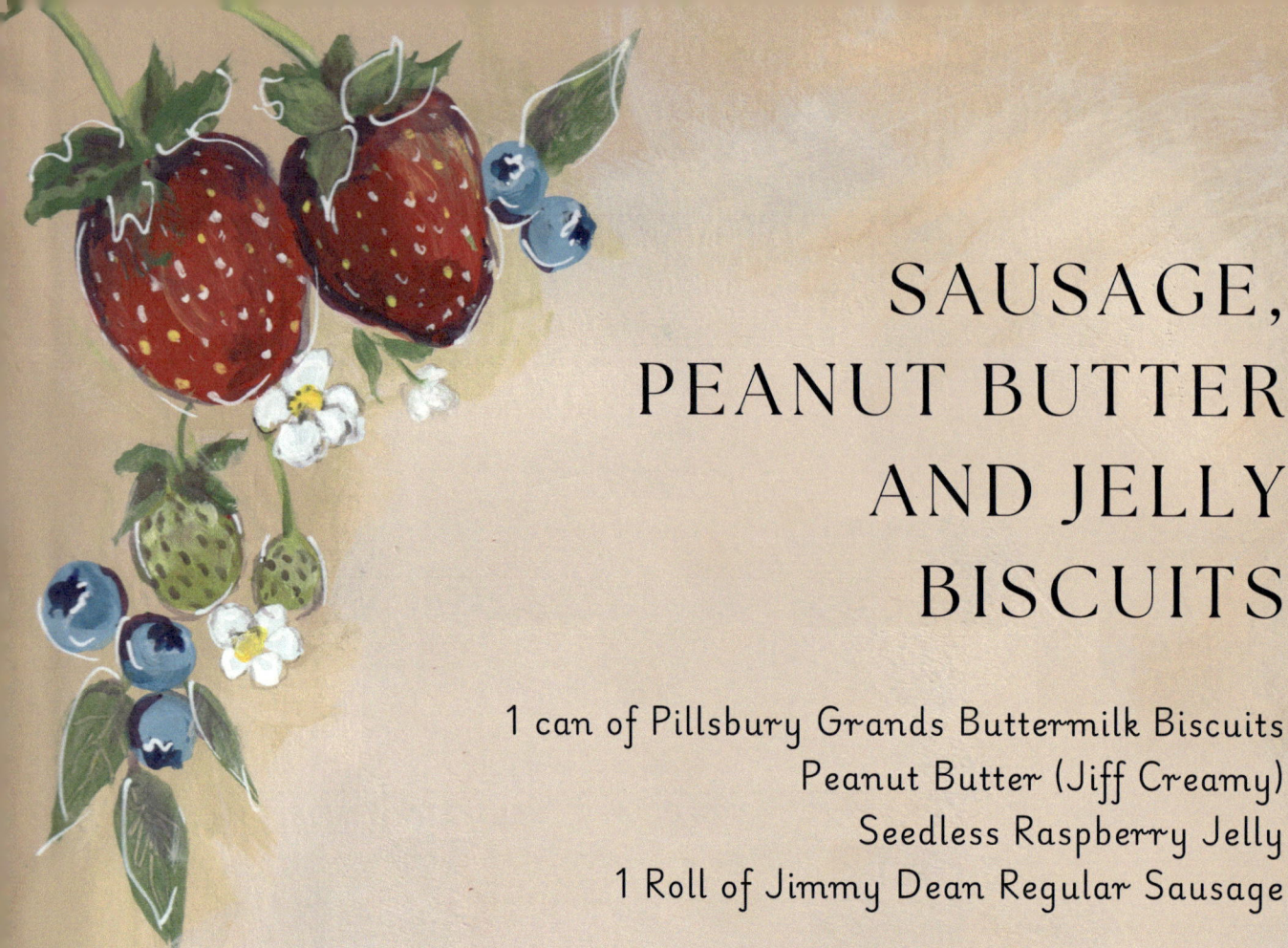

1 can of Pillsbury Grands Buttermilk Biscuits
Peanut Butter (Jiff Creamy)
Seedless Raspberry Jelly
1 Roll of Jimmy Dean Regular Sausage

- Cut sausage into slices, cook thoroughly, drain and set aside
- Bake biscuits according to package instructions. Let cool slightly. Slice in half horizontally.
- Spread 1-2 tablespoons of peanut butter on one half. Spread 1-2 tablespoons of jelly on top of the peanut butter. Add a slice of sausage. Place the biscuit half on top.

The candles shine bright
on the biscuits with jelly.
What a fun way to fill their bellies.

Breakfast by candlelight
starts the morning just right!

It's Sunday morning,
what a beautiful day.
Steve and Kelli can't wait
to go outside and play.
But before they do, you know it's true,
the glow of candlelight will start their day.
Yummy, Yummy, oh what a smell,
It's homemade cinnamon rolls,
they both could tell.
The food, the table, the candles so bright,
With a wonderful breakfast along the way.

CINNAMON ROLLS

16 oz pizza dough
2 tablespoons softened butter
3 tablespoons sugar
3 teaspoons cinnamon

- Preheat oven to 400 degrees F.
- Roll out dough on a floured surface (roll very thin, just under 1/4 inch is perfect).
- Spread the remaining ingredients on top.
- Cut long strips, then roll each up as tightly as possible.
- Put into greased baking pan.
- Bake 20 minutes.

Make the Cinnamon Roll Glaze while rolls are baking:
Mix 1 1/2 cups powdered sugar with 2-4 tablespoons of milk.
Whisk ingredients to form a glaze.
Drizzle over rolls with a spoon as soon as taken out of oven.
Serve with fresh fruit and orange juice!

Breakfast by candlelight starts every morning just right!

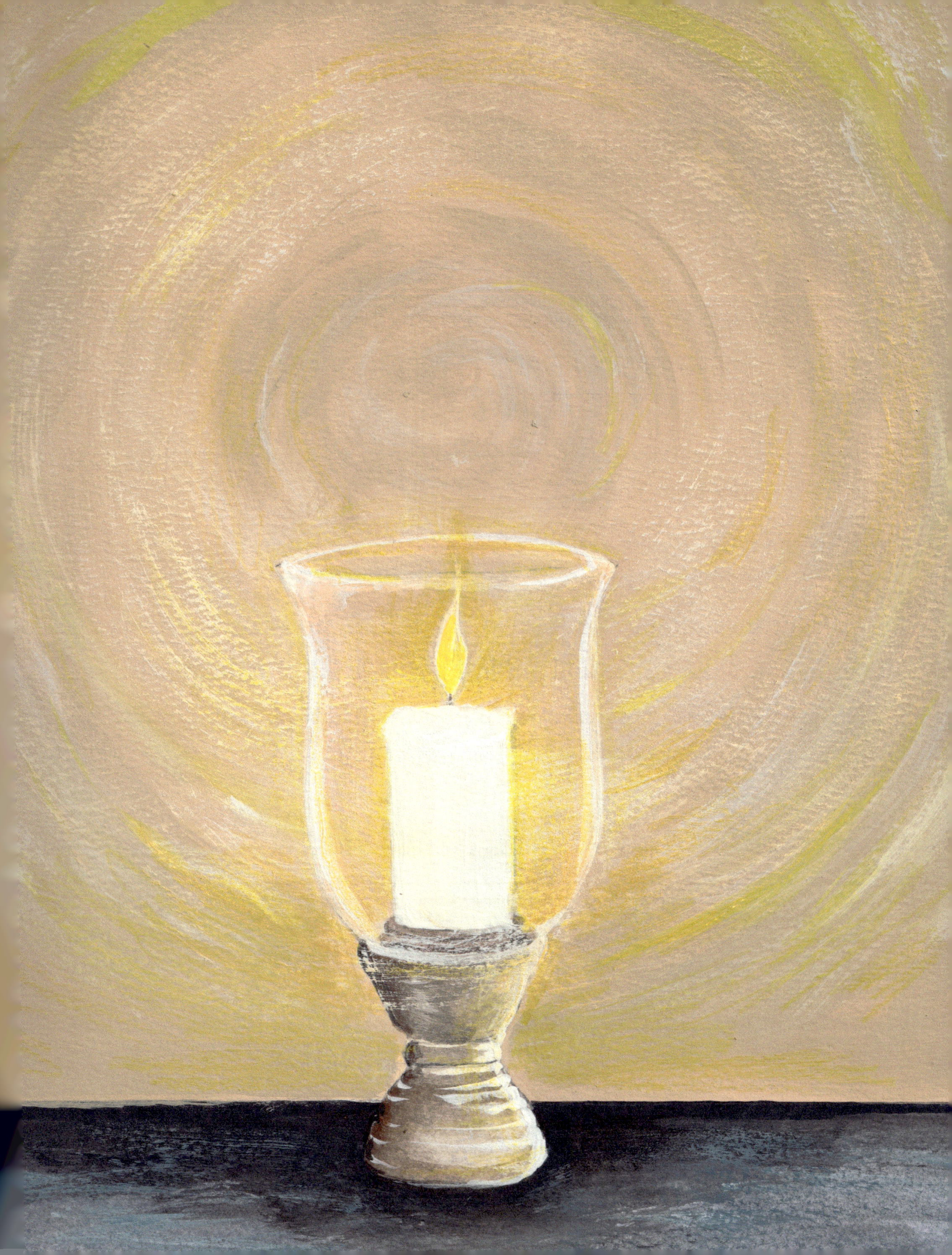

ABOUT THE AUTHOR

Lori Mattice, a Real Estate Broker, currently spends her winters in Tallahassee, Florida and summer months in Highlands, North Carolina with her husband, Bill, a retired banker. They enjoy golf, croquet, pickleball and hiking in the beautiful mountains of North Carolina. They have a blended family of 4 grown children and 10 grandchildren. This book is dedicated to Lori and Bill's son, Steve Bennett Schroeder, who passed away unexpectedly in 2023 at the age of 37. Lori has been working on her book for several years and is excited to finally have it published!

ABOUT THE ILLUSTRATOR

Jan Shannon studied art at Volunteer State Community College and O'more School of Design. In addition to this book, Jan illustrated "Mason the Lucky Dog" and "The Warrior Princess". Other works includes Heritage Quilt Barn murals displayed across rural Tennessee and more custom items can be seen at Janshannonart on Instagram. She lives with her husband Robby and has two grown children Adam and Brooke. She is also eagerly awaiting her first Grandchild in September 2024.

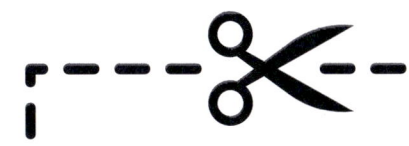

Here are the recipes from the book for your enjoyment.

Recipe for:

BLUEBERRY SMILEY FACE PANCAKES

1 cup whole wheat pancake mix
1 cup milk
1 tablespoon vegetable oil
1 egg
Fresh blueberries

Heat skillet over medium-low heat or electric griddle to 375 degrees. Combine all ingredients (except blueberries) and stir until large lumps disappear (do not overmix). Let stand for 1-2 minutes to thicken. Pour 1/4 cup of batter for each pancake onto lightly greased skillet. Arrange blueberries on top of the pancake into a smiley face. Turn when pancakes bubble and bottoms are golden brown. Serve with warm blueberry syrup and butter!

Recipe for:

HEART-TEE EGG SANDWICH

2 slices wheat or white sandwich bread (buttered on both sides)
2 eggs
Heart shaped cookie cutter
Salt and pepper to taste
Pam spray

Use cookie cutter to cut heart shape in the middle of the bread. Butter both sides of the bread. Spray Pam on skillet. Place 2 pieces of bread in skillet over medium heat. Crack egg into the heart shape in bread - cook to desired doneness. Flip the bread over and cook on the other side until golden brown. Salt and pepper to taste.
Sides: Crispy bacon and orange juice

Recipe for:

FRUIT AND YOGURT PARFAIT (4 servings)

4 tall glasses
3 cups vanilla yogurt
1 cup fresh strawberries
1/2 cup fresh blueberries
1/2 cup raspberries
1/2 cup blackberries

1/2 cup sliced bananas
1/2 cup cantaloupe cubed
1 cup good quality granola

Layer 1/3 cup vanilla yogurt in the bottom of each of the 4 tall glasses. Combine all fresh fruit (make sure all fruit is washed and sliced if necessary). Alternate layers of the fruit and granola with the yogurt until glasses are filled to the top (sprinkle additional granola on top). Serve immediately so the granola stays crunchy.

Recipe for:

FRENCH TOAST STICKS

4 slices wheat or white bread
3 eggs
1 teaspoon butter
1 tablespoon milk
Powdered sugar
Maple syrup heated

Crack 3 eggs into a mixing bowl. Add milk. Whisk eggs and milk together. Heat butter in skillet. Dip bread into egg mixture soaking egg mixture on both sides of bread. Place bread into skillet and cook French toast until golden brown on both sides. Remove from heat and cut bread into 4 sticks (slices). Place on plate, sprinkle powdered sugar over French toast sticks and dip the sticks into the warm maple syrup.

Recipe for:

CHOCOLATE CHIP WAFFLES (Makes six 4" waffles)

Waffle maker
Pam spray
Pancake Mix (wheat or white)
Ghirardelli Premium Baking Grand Sweet Chocolate Chips
Whipped cream in spray bottle
1 1/4 cups milk
1 egg
3 tablespoons vegetable oil

Heat waffle iron. Combine 1 1/4 cup pancake mix with 1 1/4 cups milk, 1 egg and 3 tablespoons vegetable oil. Stir until large clumps disappear. Allow batter to rest 4-5 minutes before baking. Pour 1/4 cup of batter into lightly greased waffle iron. Bake until steaming stops. Take waffles out of waffle iron and transfer to plate. Sprinkle chocolate chips on top of waffle followed by a few squirts of whipped cream. Serve with syrup and butter if desired.

Recipe for:

SAUSAGE, PEANUT BUTTER AND JELLY BISCUITS

1 can of Pillsbury Grands Buttermilk Biscuits
Peanut Butter (Jiff Creamy)
Seedless Raspberry Jelly
1 Roll of Jimmy Dean Regular Sausage

Cut sausage into slices, cook thoroughly, drain and set aside. Bake biscuits according to package instructions. Let cool slightly. Slice in half horizontally. Spread 1-2 tablespoons of peanut butter on one half. Spread 1-2 tablespoons of jelly on top of the peanut butter. Add a slice of sausage. Place the biscuit half on top.

Recipe for:

CINNAMON ROLLS

16 oz pizza dough
2 tablespoons softened butter
3 tablespoons sugar
3 teaspoons cinnamon

Preheat oven to 400 degrees F. Roll out dough on a floured surface (roll very thin, just under 1/4 inch is perfect). Spread the remaining ingredients on top. Cut long strips, then roll each up as tightly as possible. Put into greased baking pan. Bake 20 minutes.

Make the Cinnamon Roll Glaze while rolls are baking. Mix 1 1/2 cups powdered sugar with 2-4 tablespoons of milk. Whisk ingredients to form a glaze. Drizzle over rolls with a spoon as soon as taken out of oven. Serve with fresh fruit and orange juice!

Made in the USA
Columbia, SC
10 April 2025